21st Century
Basic Skills
Library

WE SEE SNOWFLAKES IN WINTER

by Rebecca Felix

Cherry Lake Publishing • Ann Arbor, Michigan

1

Published in the United States of America
by Cherry Lake Publishing
Ann Arbor, Michigan
www.cherrylakepublishing.com

Consultant: Marla Conn, ReadAbility, Inc.
Editorial direction and book production: Red Line Editorial

Photo Credits: Maya Kruchankova/Shutterstock Images, cover, 1; Serg Zastavkin/Shutterstock Images, 4; Max Topchii/Shutterstock Images, 6; Shutterstock Images, 8; Maieain/iStockphoto/Thinkstock, 10; borzywoj/ Shutterstock Images, 12; Mari/iStockphoto, 14; naumoid/iStockphoto, 16; Thomas M Perkins/Shutterstock Images, 18; Melbye/iStockphoto, 20

Library of Congress Cataloging-in-Publication Data
Felix, Rebecca, 1984-
  We see snowflakes in winter / by Rebecca Felix.
     pages cm -- (Let's look at winter)
  Includes index.
  Audience: 006.
  Audience: K-3.
  ISBN 978-1-63137-612-2 (hardcover) -- ISBN 978-1-63137-657-3 (pbk.)--
  ISBN 978-1-63137-702-0 (pdf ebook) -- ISBN 978-1-63137-747-1 (hosted ebook)
  1. Snowflakes--Juvenile literature. 2. Snow--Juvenile literature. 3. Winter--Juvenile literature. I. Title. II. Series: Felix, Rebecca, 1984- Let's look at winter.

  QC926.37.F45 2013
  551.57'84--dc23

                                    2014004569

Cherry Lake Publishing would like to acknowledge the work of The Partnership for 21st Century Skills. Please visit www.p21.org for more information.

Printed in the United States of America
Corporate Graphics Inc.
July 2014

TABLE OF CONTENTS

What Do You See?

What warm clothes do you see?

Cold

Winter is here.
Weather gets cold.

Air holds **water vapor** we cannot see. It **freezes** when air in the sky gets cold.

8

Ice

Ice covers dust **specks** in the sky. They become snowflakes.

The specks become heavier than air. They fall. Ice **crystals** grow on them as they fall.

Crystals grow in many **patterns**. Each snowflake is different!

Snowing

We see snowflakes fall.
We say it is snowing.

Many snowflakes fall in a winter storm. This is a snowstorm.

What Do You See?

What activity do you see?

On the Ground

Snowflakes stick together. They cover the ground.

What Do You See?

What grows in spring?

20

Soon, spring is near. Weather warms. We see snow melt.

Find Out More

BOOK

Cassino, Mark. *The Story of Snow*. San Francisco: Chronicle, 2009.

WEB SITE

Sid the Science Kid—PBS Kids
pbskids.org/sid/fablab_snowflakematch.html
Match snowflake shapes. Then watch them fall and melt.

Glossary

crystals (KRIS-tulz) things that form in flat patterns when they turn solid

freezes (FREEZ-ez) becomes solid and turns to ice

patterns (PAT-urnz) shapes that repeat and make designs

specks (SPEKS) very tiny bits

water vapor (WAW-tur VAY-pur) water in gas form

Home and School Connection

Use this list of words from the book to help your child become a better reader. Word games and writing activities can help beginning readers reinforce literacy skills.

activity	fall	near	specks
air	freezes	patterns	spring
become	ground	say	stick
clothes	grow	see	storm
cold	heavier	sky	together
cover	holds	snow	warm
crystals	ice	snowflakes	water vapor
different	many	snowing	weather
dust	melt	snowstorm	winter

What Do You See?

What Do You See? is a feature paired with select photos in this book. It encourages young readers to interact with visual images in order to build the ability to integrate content in various media formats.

You can help your child further evaluate photos in this book with additional activities. Look at the images in the book without the What Do You See? feature. Ask your child to describe one detail in each image, such as a food, activity, or setting.

Index

About the Author

Rebecca Felix is an editor and writer from Minnesota. It snows there often in winter. Snow covers the ground into spring! Rebecca likes to watch snowflakes fall from the sky.